BRIGHTON AND HOVE

A PORTRAIT IN OLD PICTURE POSTCARDS

by

David Ticehurst

S. B. Publications

To my wife Allan and son Trevor

First published in 1994 by S.B. Publications
c/o 19 Grove Road, Seaford, East Sussex, BN25 1TP

ISBN 1 85770 070 8

Typeset and Printed by Island Press Ltd.
3 Cradle Hill Industrial Estate, Seaford, East Sussex, BN25 3JE
Tel: 01323 490222

CONTENTS

CONTENTS

CONTENTS

Front Cover: Brighton and Hove Albion F.C. (1910-11).

Back Cover: Novelty postcard published by E.T.W. Dennis and Sons Ltd of London and Scarborough in their "Dainty" series.

BIBLIOGRAPHY

Tim Carder & Roger Harris   - SEAGULLS! The Story of Brighton & Hove Albion F.C. (1993)
Barry J Hugman   - Football League Players Records 1946 - 1992 (1992)
Tonie & Valmai Holt   - Picture Postcards of the Golden Age-A Collector's Guide (1978)

ACKNOWLEDGMENTS

Whilst the majority of the postcards for the illustrations in this book have been selected from the author's own collection, the author is indebted to:

Roger Harris   for the loan of the cards illustrated on pages 17 and 22 and checking my text on the subject matter of the postcards.

Brian Lund   of "Reflections of a Bygone Age" for permission to use the postcard shown on page 76.

John Daniels   of "Soccer Nostalgia" for the loan of the postcard featured on the back cover.

Keith Wales   for permiting the use of the photograph on page 80.

Steve Benz   for editing and marketing.

David Bellotti   Deputy Chairman and Chief Executive of Brighton and Hove Albion F.C. for allowing the use of the Seagull logo, and providing the Foreword.

FOREWORD

This portrait of Brighton and Hove Albion Football Club gives an incredible insight into the life and times of our club. It is a fascinating story and compulsive reading.

Seagull fans can recall (providing they are not too young!) a new signing in 1902, as well as our first match in the First Division against Arsenal in 1979. Our Manager Liam Brady, can well remember that game, for he scored for Arsenal in their 4-0 win. There is even a picture of our temporary stand (known to those of us that sometimes sat in it as the Lego Stand) put up to cater for the extra crowds.

The collection could give current Albion fans some new ideas, but it is rather unlikely we could do nowadays what happened in 1921 when car owners could drive into a motor enclosure and view the game from their car!

This book is in itself a comment on the success of Brighton and Hove Albion Football Club. Those who have compiled it deserve our thanks for bringing to us in real and vivid ways the history of the club we are privileged to share.

Seagulls!

David Bellotti
Deputy Chairman and Chief Executive
Brighton & Hove Albion Football Club

INTRODUCING PICTURE POSTCARDS

It is generally accepted that the World's first postcard was issued by the Austrian authorities on 1st October 1869 following suggestions made by Dr Emanuel Hermann. Precisely one year later, the Post Office in Britain issued their first postcard. This was non pictorial with a printed stamp. On 17th June 1872 after various representations privately printed cards were allowed but postage still needed to be prepaid by obtaining a printed stamp thereon from the Inland Revenue. It was another 22 years, on 1st September 1894 that the Post Office first permitted private publishers to produce postcards to which could be affixed an adhesive postage stamp. Thus 1994 saw the centenary of this landmark which was celebrated by events and exhibitions up and down the country.

The picture postcard though, as we know it today, first appeared in 1902 when the Post Office introduced new regulations enabling the address and the message to go on the same side of the card, allowing the other side to consist entirely of the photograph. Previously the rule was that the address only was to be on one side with the reverse for both the message and picture.

As the postage rate was only $^1/_2$d, half the letter rate, the use of postcards took off at a phenomenal rate and it has been estimated that at its peak in excess of 500 million postcards were handled by the Post Office annually. Most households kept an album and friends and relatives would send cards to add to collections. On top of this of course many millions more were purchased for their picture and were not postally used. There was a vast array of subject matter available including village and town views, actors and actresses, cats, dogs and other animals, trains, shipping and flowers to name but a few - not forgetting the well known seaside comic cards. Inevitably photographers began to capture on film local events and personalities including the football team and players.

During this period the telephone was not widely available so the postcard was a quick, reliable and inexpensive method of sending messages. The Post Office had several morning and afternoon collections and deliveries to keep pace with the vast volume of mail. With the start of World War One in 1914 the postcard craze began to wane but the biggest blow fell in 1918 when the postage rate was doubled to 1d. The use of the postcard then fell into decline but the period between 1902 and 1918 is commonly termed the "Golden Age of Postcards".

Subsequent to this cards continued to be issued but never in such quantities as during the Golden Age. Locally, the Brighton and Hove area was fortunate in the number of photographers on the scene. This led to Brighton and Hove Albion F.C. being probably the most photographed football club of the time. Early Golden Age examples were from William Avenell, Foster, Seaman and Son. Also E. Pannell issued a particularly good range of team groups, player portraits and souvenir cards. However, we are most indebted as far as local sporting events are concerned to the energetic Wiles family who continued producing postcards well beyond the Golden Age and at least up until 1938 from various addresses in Brighton and Hove. Thomas and George Wiles were brothers who issued cards individually as T.W.S. Wiles and G.A. Wiles. Postcards were also published under the names D & M Wiles, Deane Wiles and Millar, Brighton Camera Exchange, and Deane Martin and Wiles.

Attractive modern cards are now available on a whole range of topics and the beginner can build up an interesting collection with only a small outlay - and this includes football cards. Soccer cards though of the bygone age have increased in price substantially over the last few years - £10 to £15 is not uncommon for cards featuring professional teams and players and even more for rarer items.

For the serious beginner I venture to suggest the following advice to obtain the most from a fascinating hobby -

1. Make the acquaintance of your local dealer and let him/her know of your collecting interests.
2. Join your local postcard club.
3. Attend as many postcard fairs as possible on a regular basis - perseverance is the key.
4. Join any club that exists covering your specialist subject.

As far as football cards are concerned point 4 above did not apply until 1990 when Paul Macnamara was instrumental in setting up the Football Postcard Collectors Club. Membership has proved a real boon to me personally and enabled me to enhance my collection of Brighton and Hove Albion cards. Members exchange information, spare cards and contribute to a quarterly Journal.

David Ticehurst
Lancing, West Sussex.

A BRIEF HISTORY OF BRIGHTON AND HOVE ALBION F.C.

I first wish to acknowledge the huge debt I owe to Roger Harris and Tim Carder who published SEAGULLS! The Story of Brighton & Hove Albion F.C. in 1993. Their comprehensive book resulting from 12 years of detailed and meticulous research has been my constant guide and source of reference when compiling this brief history and describing the background to the postcards illustrated.

Professional football first came to the town in 1898 with the formation of Brighton United who played in the Southern League for two seasons before being disbanded. Most home games were played at Sussex County Cricket Ground in Eaton Road, Hove.

A shareholder of Brighton United, William Avenell and other supporters then founded Brighton and Hove Rangers, their home pitch being at Withdean. This was an amateur club which mainly due to financial reasons only survived one season.

Enthusiasts were still keen to bring professional soccer to the area despite some opposition and in June 1901 a new club was formed. eventually the club was named Brighton and Hove Albion. It is not now clear why "Albion" was chosen or who suggested the title. The team's first game on 7th September 1901 was a friendly against Shoreham at a pitch in Dyke Road which Brighton won 2-0. The Albion played the majority of their home matches at the County Ground and their first season in the Southern League, Division 2 was quite successful finishing in 3rd place.

In 1902 the professionals were invited to share the use of the Goldstone Ground by Hove F.C., an amateur outfit. When after two years Hove F.C. decided not to use the ground any longer the Albion became sole tenants. At the end of the 1902-03 season promotion to the Southern League, Division 1 was gained. One of the highlights of the club's early history came when as Southern League champions they took on the mighty Aston Villa, Football League Champions, for the F.A. Charity Shield on 5th September 1910 and beat them 1-0 to take the trophy.

After a break during the First World War, Brighton returned to football action and were then elevated to Football League status in 1920-21 when the Southern League, Division 1 teams formed the new Third Division. This became the Third Division (South) when a Northern Section came into existence in 1921-22.

After a couple of poor seasons Brighton found their feet and played some consistent football. Over the next 17 seasons up to World War Two, the team finished in the top ten in all bar 2 campaigns without though achieving that important top spot. With only one promotion place available it was not easy to move up a Division. During this period the Albion also built up a reputation as difficult F.A. Cup opposition and accounted for a number of Division 1 teams to prove it, including Everton, Portsmouth and Chelsea.

Following the Second World War Brighton continued their lengthy stay in Division 3 (South) and also suffered the embarrassment of needing to seek re-election after finishing bottom of the table in 1947-48. Albion were runners-up after excellent seasons in 1953-54 and 1955-56 and finally managed that elusive top place in 1957-58 with a resounding 6-0 home win over Watford in the final fixture. They had succeeded in the final season of the existence of the Third Division (South). Thereafter the regional North and South divisions were reorganised into the Third and Fourth divisions.

The Albion lost their first ever match in the Second Division 9-0 at Middlesbrough but recovered to finish in a respectable 12th place. However the team never really established itself in this Division. Manager Billy Lane resigned in May 1961 after 10 years in charge. Under new boss George Curtis Brighton were relegated to Division 3 at the end of the 1961-62 season. Worse was to follow when a year later they were demoted to Division 4. Albion bounced back in 1964-65 partly thanks to a big name signing by manager Archie Macaulay. Bobby Smith, the ex-Spurs and England centre-forward, scored 20 of Brighton's 102 league goals as they were promoted as champions with an average home gate in excess of 17,000.

The next seven seasons were spent in Division 3 until promotion to Division 2 was achieved under manager Pat Saward at the end of the 1971-72 campaign. This though proved to be only a brief spell in higher company as 1972-73 saw Brighton finish bottom and relegated back to Division 3.

The next milestone was when chairman Mike Bamber sensationally acquired the services in November 1973 of Brian Clough and Peter Taylor who had just resigned from Derby County. Massive team rebuilding followed after heavy league and cup defeats at the Goldstone. Although Brian Clough left to manage Leeds United in July 1974 Peter Taylor remained to continue the rebuilding. The 1975-76 season saw his efforts nearly pay off as the Seagulls finished fourth - just one place away from promotion. Peter Taylor resigned in the close season to rejoin Brian Clough who was now in charge at Nottingham Forest.

Enter Alan Mullery to his first managerial post in which he steered Albion to promotion to Division 2 as runners-up for 1976-77. With more signings, in particular young Mark Lawrenson from Preston North End, the team nearly progressed to Division 1 at the very first attempt. Not to be denied promotion to Division 1 was gained at the end of the following season 1978-79 with a 3-1 win over Newcastle United at St. James Park in the final match of the season, with goals from Brian Horton, Peter Ward and Gerry Ryan.

Brighton enjoyed four seasons in the top flight and although relegated in 1982-83 the fans had the consolation of savouring the Seagulls only appearance in a F.A. Cup final. The first game ended in a 2-2 draw in an incident packed game against Manchester United which went to extra time. Albion were well beaten though in the replay with a 4-0 reverse.

Another four seasons in Division 2 and it was relegation blues once more at the end of 1986-87. Albion returned though with an automatic promotion place in 1987-88 which was Barry Lloyd's first full season in charge. In 1990-91 the Seagulls returned to Wembley with over 30,000 of their supporters after reaching the play-off finals. Only 90 minutes from a return to Division 1 but it was not to be as Notts County triumphed 3-1. This seemed to be a turning point. Selling star players to raise money saw the Albion in the next season slide into the relegation zone. The 1992-93 season Brighton were still in Division 2 but only because of the renaming of Division 3 after the formation of the Premier League.

Money was becoming tighter than ever and several appearances in the High Court were necessary to fend off winding up petitions. Barry Lloyd became managing director as well as manager. These financial activities amidst a search for a new ground proved an impossible task to combine with team duties. Eventually towards the end of 1993 Chairman Greg Stanley pumped more funds into the Club and David Bellotti was appointed as Chief Executive. With the team at the wrong end of the table Barry Lloyd soon departed and his successor was Liam Brady, the ex-Arsenal star and Republic of Ireland international. The tide turned almost at once. Performances improved, spectators returned and relegation fears dissolved leaving an air of optimism for the future.

WILLIAM LONGAIR, c.1899

William Longair, a Scottish International, captained Brighton United in their first ever competitive match in the Southern League Division I on 8th September 1898. The venue was the Dell - the first game ever held at Saint's new stadium. Southampton won the match 4-1 in front of 8,000 spectators. William Longair was one of seven Dundee players to move south to sign for the newly formed club. Brighton United were to play only two seasons before folding.

W. Avenell & Co   48, WEST STREET
                        BRIGHTON.

J. JACKSON   RUSHTON.   HOWES, CAMERON, H. R. BAKER. LAMB, WHITEHURST, TAYLOR, SWEETMAN, BROWN
Sec. and Manager).   COLES.   McATEER.   BOULTON.   GARFIELD.   HULME.   *(Trainer).*
HYDE.   ROBERTS.   SCOTT.   THAIR.   PADDINGTON.

BRIGHTON AND HOVE ALBION, 1903-4.

BRIGHTON AND HOVE ALBION, 1903-4

An early team group, a season before the club were to change to their familiar blue and white striped shirts. The Albion had gained promotion at the end of the 1902-3 season from Division 2 to Division 1 of the Southern League. In a better class of football the team struggled although home attendances doubled. Brighton finished 17th out of 18 teams and were lucky to be re-elected to Division 1 for the following season.

WILLIAM ROBERTS, c.1904

Billy Roberts, a skillful ball player, was signed from Grays United following previous fine performances against the Albion. Billy scored 17 goals for Brighton in 73 Southern League and FA Cup appearances from 1903-05. The photographer William Avenell was a shareholder in Brighton United, the forerunners of Brighton and Hove Albion.

COPYRIGHT.   E. PANNELL, HOVE.

BRIGHTON & HOVE ALBION FOOTBALL CLUB, 1905-6.
ENGLISH CUP TEAM.

J. Clayton (Trainer)   T. Turner   H. Kent   P. Scott Walford (Asst. Manager)   M. Mellors   E. Clare   F. Buckley   R. Kett (Manager)
C. Buckley   P. Hall   R. Joynes   W. Yates   T. Allsopp   J. Kennedy
W. Anthony   A. Fisher (Captain)   A. Fisher

BRIGHTON AND HOVE ALBION, 1905-6

Lots of new faces appeared in the team line-up for this season. Newcomers included Tom Turner from Blantyre, Frank Buckley from Aston Villa and his brother Chris signed from Manchester City. Two captures from Newark were Dick Joynes and Harry Kent whilst Albert Fisher moved from Bristol City plus Tom Allsopp, Walter Anthony and Proctor Hall came via Leicester Fosse, Nottingham Forest and Manchester United respectively. The influx of players did not bring success and the team struggled for most of the season finishing just outside the relegation zone in 16th place in Southern League Division 1. There was though a good run in the English Cup with wins against Glossop from Division 2 of the Football League and Swindon before going out to First Division Middlesbrough after two replays.

ARTHUR HULME, c1905

Arthur signed from Bristol Rovers in the summer of 1902. A very popular player who made 174 appearances for Brighton and gave sterling service to the club for 7 years. On 27th November 1907 was awarded the proceeds of a home Western League match against Southampton as a benefit for his long service. The Albion won this game 3-0. Arthur was killed in action during the First World War.

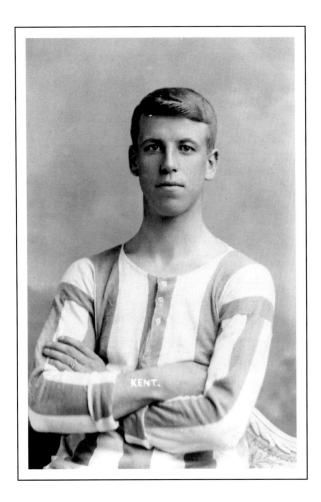

HARRY KENT, c1905

Harry, a half-back, one of the two signings from Newark in 1905 was appointed club captain the following year. His transfer in 1908 occurred in unusual circumstances. Middlesbrough wanted to sign the Albion player Jack Hall for £700 but the maximum transfer fee was £350 so they took Harry Kent as well. This limit on transfer fees was rescinded after only three months. Harry had played over 150 games for Brighton.

SIR GEORGE ROBEY

A self-portrait caricature by George Robey, the famous star of music hall who was nicknamed the "Prime Minister of Mirth". George was an excellent footballer who guested for Brighton on two occasions in friendly matches in 1903 and 1907. He scored in both games. He also played for Millwall, Chelsea and Fulham as well as arranging and playing in many charity matches. George was knighted in the New Years Honours List of 1954 but died later that year on 29th November at his home in Hove at the age of 85.

J. CLAYTON.

JOSEPH CLAYTON, c1907
Joe Clayton was the Albion trainer from the start of the 1905-6 season, replacing J. Ryder, having previously served Portsmouth in the same capacity. He was also trainer to the Sussex County Cricket Club. At the beginning of 1909-10 campaign Alf Nelmes took over from Joe as the Brighton trainer.

BRIGHTON AND HOVE ALBION, 1907-8

The 1906-7 campaign was very successful with Brighton finishing 3rd in Division 1 of the Southern League, but the team were unable to maintain this form in the following 1907-8 season slipping down to 17th place mainly because of poor away form. There were exciting moments in the English Cup. Preston North End from the First Division of the Football League were defeated 1-0 at the third attempt after a 1-1 draw at the Goldstone and a replay. In the second round another strong Football League side, Liverpool, were held to a 1-1 draw at Anfield. Although Brighton lost 3-0 in the replay a record 12,000 crowd helped the club finish the season with a healthy profit.

Brighton and Hove Football Ground.

THE GOLDSTONE GROUND, c.1908

This card shows the Goldstone Ground from behind the South Stand and was taken around 1908. The small West Stand remained until it was demolished at the end of the 1957-58 season just after the Albion had won promotion to the Second Division for the first time in their history. The large chimney to the north is the old Goldstone waterworks which still remains today but now houses the British Engineerium. Brighton and Hove Albion moved to this ground in 1902 and it is still their home today although planning permission has been granted for commercial development and a new site for a stadium is being sought.

49207. HOVE, NEW PARK SHOWING DRUIDS ALTAR.

"THE GOLD-STONE"

A postcard of the Druids Altar in Hove Park just across the road from the football ground. Local legend has it that the devil once kicked this large boulder from the Devil's Dyke in a fit of temper. It was so popular with sightseers that the farmer on whose land it was situated was forced to bury the object. More commonly known as the "Gold-Stone" it was dug up again many years later and placed in Hove Park when it opened in 1906. The trees in the park were decimated by the 1987 hurricane but the stone from which Brighton and Hove Albion's ground takes its name remains firmly in place.

BRIGHTON FOOTBALL GROUND, c.1909
This early action shot of an unidentified game at the Goldstone Ground shows the South Stand, a wooden structure purchased in 1904 from an agricultural show being held in Preston Park, Brighton which seated 1,800. It remained in place until 1949 when it was refurbished and moved back behind terracing. The stand was finally demolished and replaced in 1954.

CHARLIE WEBB, c.1910

An amateur from Worthing, Charlie Webb played the first of his 275 games for Brighton on 2nd January 1909 and marked his debut with a goal. He also scored the goal that won the F.A. Charity Shield in September 1910. An Irish international, it was though as manager for 28 years that Charlie will be best remembered. It is a measure of the respect in which he was held throughout football that Arsenal and Portsmouth came to the Goldstone to play each other in a testimonial match in September 1949. The match programme contained glowing tributes from amongst others Sir Stanley Rous, Secretary of the Football Association, Tom Whittaker and George Allison of Arsenal.

CUP-TIE SOUVENIR, 15th January 1910

An attractive souvenir postcard to commemorate the visit of Southampton to the Goldstone for round one of the English Cup. A 10,000 crowd watched Albion go down 1-0 at the first hurdle. A notable absentee from the cup-tie lineup was Bill "Bullet" Jones who was serving a two month suspension after being sent off on 1st December 1909 in a home league match against Norwich. The compensation for supporters for the defeat at the hands of the Saints was that Brighton went on to clinch the 1909-10 Southern League Division 1 title by 5 points from Swindon Town.

ALBION V PLYMOUTH ARGYLE. FEB 26 1910. A LARGE CROWD. (2) WILES HOVE

BRIGHTON v. PLYMOUTH, 26th February 1910

Not unexpectedly there was a good turn out of 6,000 fans for the home game against Plymouth. Brighton were top of the Southern League Division 1 at the time. The match ended in a 1-0 win for the home side with a second half goal from Harry Middleton. The full line-up was - Bob Whiting, Fred Blackman, Joe Leeming, Billy Booth, Joe McGhie, Jack Haworth, Bert Longstaff, Jimmy Coleman, Harry Middleton, Charlie Webb and Bill Hastings. The Albion maintained the top spot for the rest of the season and finished as champions.

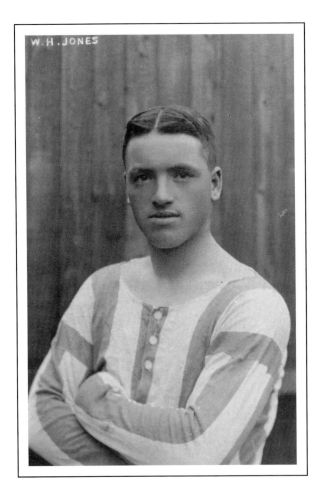

W.H.JONES

WILLIAM H. JONES, c.1910

Bill Jones joined Brighton in the summer of 1909 from Birmingham. A forward, only 5'5" tall he had a tremendous shot hence he gained the nickname "Bullet". In his first season with the Albion he was top scorer for the club with 22 goals despite a two month suspension. The following season 1910-11 Bill was again the leading Albion marksman. He returned to the Birmingham club in 1912 for a £300 transfer fee but was back in Brighton colours in 1913 and remained playing until 1920 when he was appointed assistant trainer. "Bullet" made a total of 179 first team appearances for the Albion and scored 69 goals.

BRIGHTON AND HOVE ALBION MOOCHERS, 1910-11
In the years leading to the Great War novelty postcards were often produced by local photographers which proved very popular with the public. Taken during the 1910-11 season, this photo shows the Albion "Moochers" with a variety of props. Line-up left to right -
Back row: Joe Lumley, Joe Leeming, Billy Booth, Ralph Routledge, Jimmy Smith.
Seated: Jack Haworth, Tom Wake, Jimmy Coleman,
unknown, Harry Middleton, Billy Miller, Bob Whiting.

BRIGHTON AND HOVE ALBION, 1910-11

A proud team group showing it's various achievements. The Southern League Challenge Shield was the trophy for winning the Division 1 title the previous season. This campaign had seen the Albion gain 59 points from 42 matches scoring 69 goals and only conceding 28. The Southern Charity Cup was also won in the 1909-10 season by beating Watford 1-0 in the final at Stamford Bridge on 4th April 1910. As Southern League Champions Brighton qualified to meet Aston Villa, the Football League victors, again at Chelsea's ground on 5th September 1910 for the Charity Shield. Against all the odds the Albion triumphed 1-0 with a goal from Charlie Webb after 72 minutes.

BRIGHTON v. QUEENS PARK RANGERS, 29th October 1910
Part of the 8,000 crowd snapped at the South Stand end of the ground ready for kick-off in the Southern
League Division 1 fixture between Brighton and QPR. The Albion were league leaders at the time and
won this match 2-1 with goals from Charlie Webb and Jimmy Coleman. All three goals came in the first
half. A week earlier the Albion had been away at Millwall for the opening league game at their new
ground "The Den". Brighton spoilt the party for 25,000 spectators by winning 1-0. Jack Haworth scored
the only goal after 82 minutes.

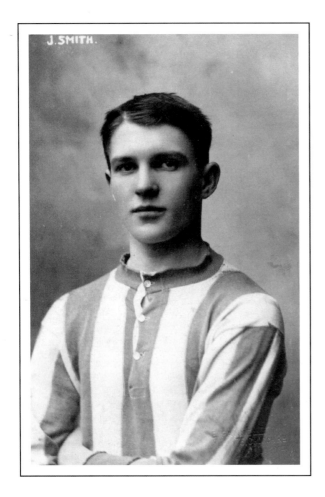

J.SMITH.

JIMMY SMITH, c.1911

A big impact was made by Jimmy Smith in only a short period with Brighton. Jimmy was signed from Hanley in January 1911 and in 65 games scored 40 goals. In November 1912 the Albion were unable to afford to turn down an offer of £735 cash plus player Bobby Simpson from Bradford Park Avenue and his goal scoring abilities were subsequently greatly missed.

ALBION 5
SAINTS 0

WILES
HOVE (5)

ALBION V SOUTHAMPTON · HOVE · OCT 7, 1911. "BILLY BOOTH'S FIRST GOAL FOR THE ALBIONS.

BRIGHTON v SOUTHAMPTON, 7th October 1911

A superb Albion performance to make up for the depressing weather. The rain kept the gate down to 4,000 for this Southern League Division 1 fixture. Many spectators must have regretted their absence as Brighton stormed to a 5-0 half-time lead with goals from Billy Booth, Archie Needham (2) and Charlie Webb (2). The Albion could not add to their tally in the second period but ran out comfortable winners. Brighton finished fifth in the table thanks to impressive home form with 15 victories, 2 draws and only 2 reverses at the Goldstone Ground.

ALBION CRICKET TEAM, 1912

Over the years Albion have played cricket matches against a variety of local sides with some success. This postcard commemorates a fixture with a team from the recently formed Supporters' Club at Preston Park in 1912. Line-up left to right -

Back row: unknown, Alf Nelmes (trainer), Jimmy Smith, Archie Needham, Jack Woodhouse, Billy Booth, unknown, Fred Goodwin.

Seated: Billy Middleton, Ralph Routledge, Fred Coles (assistant trainer), Bob Whiting, Billy Miller, Tom Wake, Jack Robson (manager).

WILLIAM MILLER, c.1912

Bill Miller made his debut for Brighton on 10th September 1910 in an away game at Watford which Albion lost 2-1. Although not a first team regular Bill did hit the net 13 times in 21 Southern League matches in 1913-14 which made him top goal scorer. During the War he served with the Sussex Volunteer Regiment together with clubmates George Coomber and Fred Eacock. His final first team appearance was in a 1-0 defeat at Northampton. In recognition of his loyalty Bill was awarded a joint testimonial match with Bert Longstaff in 1923.

W. MILLER.

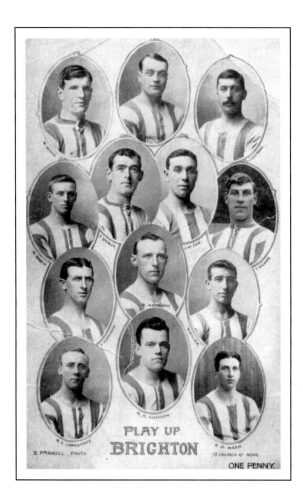

PLAY UP BRIGHTON, c.1912
Another of the cameo type popular postcards issued during the 1912-13 season. Frank Spencer was a new recruit from the Parkside club, South Shields, who as a full-back went on to play over 140 games for Brighton. The season was notable for the formation at Brighton's suggestion of a Southern Alliance League to run alongside the Southern League. The rules of the new competition stipulated that each club field a minimum of seven first-team regulars. The Albion finished as runners-up to Croydon Common in this first Southern Alliance League but went one better to win the trophy in 1913-14 after which they withdrew from the competition due to poor attendances for such matches.

CUP-TIE SPECIAL, 11th January 1913

Albion supporters photographed before joining the motor coach at Hove Station for the journey to Fratton Park on 11th January 1913 for the first round of the English Cup game against Portsmouth. Unfortunately the travelling fans were to be disappointed as the match was postponed. The game did take place the following Wednesday, 15th January when Brighton won 2-1 before a crowd of 15,556. The reward was a home tie with Everton which was drawn 0-0, Albion going out of the competition in the replay at Goodison Park 0-1 after extra time.

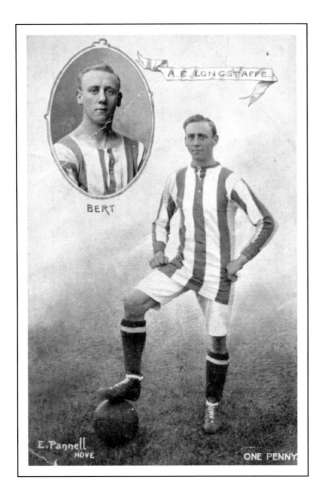

ALBERT LONGSTAFF,
16th April 1913

Born and bred in Shoreham, West Sussex, Bert Longstaff signed as a professional with Brighton and Hove Albion on 24th October 1907. The above postcard which spells Bert's surname incorrectly was issued on the occasion of his benefit against Portsmouth in a Southern Alliance match at the Goldstone which the home team won 3-0 with goals from Bill Miller, Jack Woodhouse and appropriately the beneficiary. Bert was a wonderful servant to the club and made 443 appearances, the last of which was on 22nd October 1921 when the Albion lost 1-0 at Charlton in a Football League Division 3 (South) fixture. A well deserved second benefit match jointly with Bill Miller was held on 5th May 1923.

26

BRIGHTON v. SWINDON, 26th April 1913

The above postcard shows action from the Southern League Division 1 match at the Goldstone when the opposition was Swindon Town. This was a very important game for the visitors as it was their last fixture of the 1912-13 season and they desperately needed both points from a victory to stand any chance of becoming league champions. In the event Brighton gained an excellent 2-0 win with first half goals from Jack Woodhouse and Bobby Simpson. Swindon had to settle for runners-up spot behind Plymouth Argyle.

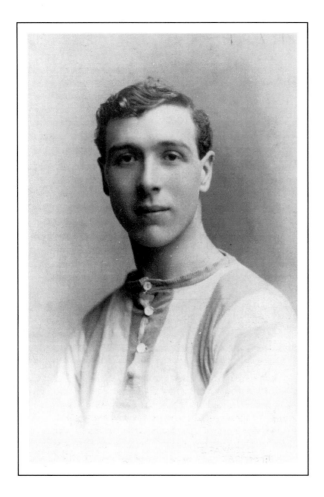

ALFIE TYLER, c.1913
Alfie Tyler played 69 first team games for Brighton in the period 1913-15 after joining the club from East Grinstead. A left winger, his only goal for the Albion was in the away match against Plymouth Argyle in a Southern League Division 1 game on 20th December 1913. In common with many other footballers of that era his career was cut short by the Great War.

The Albion's English Cup Record Jan 31. 1914

RECORD GATE 15.727
RECORD RECEIPTS £990.18.6
RECORD ENTRY INTO
          THIRD ROUND
OLDHAM ATHELTIC ~ ALBION
          1 - 1
ALBION ~ OLDHAM (Replay)
          1 - 0
ALBION ~ CLAPTON ORIENT
          3 - 1

E. PANNELL
HOVE
(Copyright)

JOE LEEMING
LEADING HIS MEN TO VICTORY

A. GOODWIN

CUP-TIE SOUVENIR, 31st January 1914

Brighton had built up a good reputation in the English Cup (now the FA Cup). In the first round on 10th January 1914 Oldham, who were near the top of the Football League Division 1, fielded a team with several international players. Oldham were 1-0 up at half time but Bill Miller equalised for the Albion twelve minutes from the end. The replay at the Goldstone went into extra time but Brighton clinched the tie with a goal by Billy Booth with minutes remaining to the delight of the 10,700 crowd. As the above card shows the next round brought a record gate and receipts. Clapton Orient were leading 1-0 at the midway point but a strong second half performance saw Albion emerge as 3-1 winners with goals from Charlie Webb (2) and Bullet Jones. In the next round Brighton were drawn away against Sheffield Wednesday but lost 3-0 despite holding their powerful opponents 0-0 at half time.

POM POM· BRIGHTON'S GOALIE WHO AMUSED THE CROWDS BY HIS LONG KICKS. (FEB·28·1914) BRIGHTON V PORTSMOUTH· GOLDSTONE GROUND·HOVE·

BOB WHITING, 1914

Bob "Pom Pom" Whiting played over 300 games in goal for Brighton from 1908-1915. Bob joined the Albion on transfer from Chelsea. Unfortunately this Brighton stalwart was killed on active duty during the First World War. The match mentioned a side against Portsmouth on 28th February 1914 was a Southern League Division 1 fixture which ended in a 3-2 win for the Albion in front of around 6,000 fans. Brighton's goals came from Bert Longstaff (2) and George Dodd.

BRIGHTON AND HOVE ALBION, 1914-15

The First World War had started and the season saw reduced crowds amid the feeling that the players should be fighting for their country not playing football. The Albion finished in tenth place in Division 1 of the Southern League after a poor run in. At the end of the season the club directors decided to close down until the cessation of hostilities. From the team photograph above Charlie Matthews, Jasper Batey, Bob Whiting, Charlie Dexter and Ernie Townsend were to lose their lives during the War. Groundsman Fred Bates also perished in the conflict.

Albion Sharp Shooters.

BRIGHTON RIFLE DRILL, c.1914

This postcard shows the Brighton team doing rifle drill in the early months of the War. In the following few months most of the players had signed up for the Footballers Battalion of the Middlesex Regiment. A miniature range was erected at the Goldstone Ground and the players drilled and practised under the command of Charlie Webb, a player and future manager, who had been a regular soldier. In one incident a group of bored players decided to take pot shots at some crows. Unfortunately a director's house overlooked the ground and he had been watching at the window when bullets intended for crows whistled past his head. He was not amused and the culprits were fined.

BRIGHTON HALF BACK LINE, 1920

These three long-serving players clocked up 800 first team appearances between them although Billy Booth and Tom "Gunner" Higham both departed at the close of the 1919-20 season which marked the end of an era. The following season 1920-21 saw the formation of the Third Division of the Football League which was made up of clubs in the Southern League Division 1. Billy Booth had been signed from Sheffield United in 1908 and Gunner Higham arrived a few months earlier. George Coomber had joined as an amateur from Tufnell Park in 1913. George retired in 1925 after injury. Later he ran a local building contractors and did much work at the Goldstone for his old club free of charge.

W·BOOTH — G·COOMBER — T·E·HIGHAM.

BRIGHTON & HOVE ALBION. HALF BACK LINE·1920.

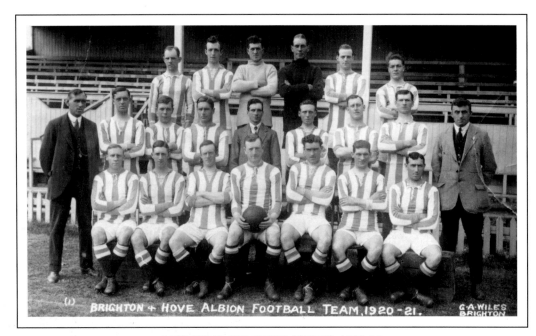

BRIGHTON AND HOVE ALBION, 1920-21

The First Division teams of the Southern League formed the basis of the new Football League Division 3 (South) from 1920-21. Brighton's first home match was on 1st September 1920 when Merthyr Town visited the Goldstone. The game was drawn 0-0. The Albion finished this first season 18th out of 22 teams. The above postcard shows (left to right) -

Back row: Dave Williams, Wally Little, Ossie Randall, Billy Hayes, Tom Brown, unknown.

Middle row: Alf Nelmes (trainer), George Coomber, unknown, Jack Woodhouse, Charlie Webb (manager), Zacky March, Harry Bentley, Jack Burnham, Dickie Meades (asst. trainer).

Front row: Bert Longstaff, Fretwell Hall, George Ritchie, Jack Rutherford (captain), Jack Doran, Ted Rodgerson, Billy Miller.

ANDREW NEIL, 1920-21
Andy Neil, a forward, made his debut for Brighton on Christmas Day 1920 in a Division 3 (South) game at the Goldstone versus Crystal Palace. The crowd of 14,000 saw Albion succumb 2-0 to their near rivals. Andy was transferred to Arsenal in March 1924, an acquisition which cost the Gunners £3,000. He rejoined Brighton in March 1926 but left the club again in the summer of 1927. During his spells at the Albion Andy played 185 first team games scoring 30 goals.

CUP-TIE SOUVENIR,
8th January 1921

First Division Oldham were the opposition in the first round of the English Cup at the Goldstone Ground. A then record crowd of 16,972 saw Brighton storm to a convincing 4-1 victory with goals from Zacky March (2), Jack Doran and George Coomber. In the next round Cardiff City visited the Goldstone when a new record attendance of 20,260 was set. The game ended in a goalless draw and unfortunately Albion's Jack Bollington broke his leg, an injury that ended his career. Cardiff won the replay 1-0.

BRIGHTON v. WATFORD, 1920-21

This action took place on 30th April 1921 and was in fact a Southern League fixture between the reserve sides of both clubs, the first elevens being in the newly formed Football League Division 3 (South). Dave Williams, the scorer, went on to win a medal as a member of the Albion team that took the Southern League championship (English Section) that season. The reserve side was nicknamed the "Lambs". The card does also illustrate the prodigious output of the photographers who covered reserve team and other matches at the Goldstone as well as first team fixtures.

JACK DORAN, 1921

Brighton had signed George Holley, the ex-Sunderland and England forward, but injury cut short his career after only 13 appearances. Jack Doran was signed from Norwich as a replacement and made an immediate impact which also brought international recognition. He was transferred to Manchester City in August 1922 for £1,050 after scoring 55 goals for the Albion in 85 games. Jack's most prolific period was at the start of the 1921-22 season when he hit the target 17 times in 14 matches, which included two hat-tricks and five goals in the 7-0 home victory over Northampton.

BRIGHTON v. SOUTHEND, 27th August 1921

The more affluent supporters were able to bring their motor cars into a special enclosure on match days. The above postcard shows the lucky few at the opening fixture of the 1921-22 campaign in Division 3 (South). The game finished in a 0-0 draw before 13,500 fans.

CHRISTMAS GREETINGS, 1922

This Christmas card was issued at a time when the club's fortunes on the playing front were improving. The team ensured that their supporters had a splendid festive period by defeating South Coast rivals, Portsmouth, 7-1 at the Goldstone on the 25th December before a 15,000 crowd in a Football League, Division 3 (South) match. The return fixture at Fratton Park on Boxing Day was also won by the Albion, by the closer margin of 2-1. This good form continued into the New Year and Brighton finished in fourth spot in the table.

BRIGHTON AND HOVE ALBION, 1922-23

In the official team group for this season the players, manager, trainer and assistant trainer look very serious. This postcard of just the players shows them in lighter mood. Brighton went on to finish fourth in Division 3 (South) that season, fifteen places higher than the previous year. The above line-up (left to right) is -

Back row: Jack Thompson, Jack Jenkins, H. Baker, Billy Hayes, Reg Phillips.
Middle row: Edgar Saunders, Jack Woodhouse, George Coomber, George Moorhead, Wally Little, Jimmy Jones.
Front row: Jack Nightingale, Abe Jones, Billy McAllister, Andy Neil, Jack Feebery (captain), Fred Groves, Jimmy Moore, Tug Wilson, Arnold Broadhead.

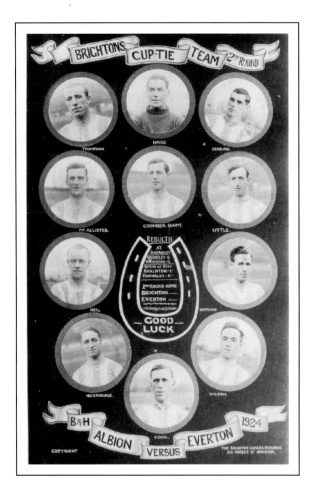

CUP-TIE SOUVENIR, 2nd February 1924

In the English Cup the Albion had conquered Second Division Barnsley, after a replay at the Goldstone when a 22,066 crowd watched Jimmy Hopkins score a late goal. This earned an attractive home tie against an illustrious Everton side from the First Division. A gate of 27,450 saw Brighton cause one of the upsets of the season by winning 5-2 with a hat-trick by Tommy Cook and other goals from Wally Little (penalty) and Andy Neil. Their reward was a third round meeting with Manchester City.

BRIGHTON v. MANCHESTER CITY, 23rd February 1924

Hoping for a repeat of the cup exploits against Barnsley and Everton, this postcard shows part of the 24,734 crowd in front of the South Stand for the third round English Cup match against Manchester City. However, Albion were unable to continue the giant-killing and City cruised to a 5-1 victory at the Goldstone. The away side included Billy Meredith playing just a few months before his fiftieth birthday. The numbered sign was to enable spectators to identify the postcard in the photographers window after the game.

WILSON · BRIGHTON + HOVE ALBION · F.C. 1925·6

ERNIE WILSON, 1925-26

In May 1922 Ernie "Tug" Wilson was signed from Denaby United. What a capture this proved to be as the popular character went on to play over 560 games for the Albion. A left-winger, 509 of these appearances were in the League (67 goals) which is a club record. Tug played his last match on 13th April 1936 in a home Division 3 (South) fixture against Millwall which ended 0-0. After retirement from the first class game he played locally in Sussex County League football.

TOMMY COOK, 1925-26

Tommy played 209 League and Cup games for Brighton, finding the net on 123 occasions. His goal tally earned an England cap in 1924-25, a rare distinction for a Third Division player. He made his Albion debut on 23rd September 1922 in a goalless draw at Queens Park Rangers and bowed out against Walsall on 1st May 1929, scoring in the 2-1 home victory. Tommy was also a fine all-round cricketer who played regularly for Sussex. His top innings was 278 in July 1930 against Hampshire. There was a brief return to the Goldstone as manager in 1947, before his death three years later.

T. COOK · B & H. ALBION F.C. 1925 + 6
WEARING HIS ENGLISH INTERNATIONAL CAP + JERSEY.

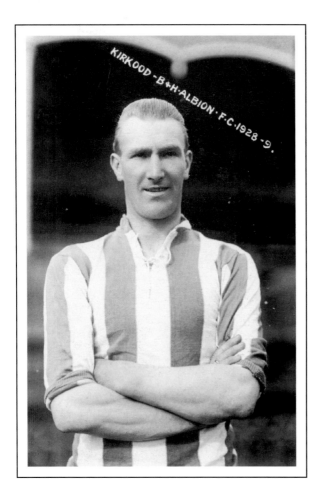

DAN KIRKWOOD, 1928-29

Dan Kirkwood joined Brighton from Sheffield Wednesday in 1928 and was an immediate success scoring 20 goals in 40 Division 3 (South) appearances in the first season. The defence conceded lots of goals though and the end of the 1928-29 campaign saw Albion in 15th place. Crowds slumped and on 2nd February 1929 the smallest gate at the Goldstone, 2,093, was recorded. The faithful few were rewarded with a 3-0 victory over Norwich City and saw goals from Dan Kirkwood, Bobby Farrell and Tug Wilson. Dan went on to record 181 appearances (82 goals) before his transfer to Luton Town in October 1933.

HUGH VALLANCE, 1929-30

Although only with Brighton for little over a season, the name Hugh Vallance remained on the record books as top goalscorer with 32 (1929-30) until eclipsed by Peter Ward's 36 in 1976-77. Born in Wolverhampton Hugh, who had previously been with Aston Villa and Queens Park Rangers, forged a great partnership with Dan Kirkwood as Brighton amassed 87 league goals. In October 1930 Hugh, together with Jack Curran, was sensationally sacked by the Albion for undisclosed offences and subsequently continued his football career with various clubs including Gillingham and a spell in France.

T. POTTER SMITH, c.1929

An excellent signing from Cardiff City before the start of the 1929-30 season, Potter Smith went on to make in excess of 300 appearances for the Albion. He was appointed club captain for 1935 to 1937 before hanging up his boots at the end of 1936-37, which saw Brighton finish the season third in Division 3 (South) behind Luton Town and Notts County.

DAVE WALKER, c.1929

Another astute signing, this time from Walsall, half-back Dave Walker made 349 appearances for Brighton. Joining the club at the start of the 1929-30 season he played for ten years before retiring from the game. Was awarded a testimonial match on 28th April 1937 in an Albion v. Southampton encounter which ended in a 1-1 draw.

**CUP-TIE SOUVENIR,
15th February 1930**

The club were once again in poor financial shape so a good cup run was essential and the team did not disappoint. Having accounted for Southern League opposition in the first two rounds of the F.A. Cup, the Albion faced First Division outfits in rounds 3 and 4. Both matches at Grimsby (a replay after a 1-1 draw at the Goldstone) and Portsmouth ended 1-0 to Brighton on each occasion, the winner being scored by Hugh Vallance. Another away tie against First Division Newcastle followed and a massive 56,469 crowd saw the Magpies triumph 3-0 with a hat-trick from Hughie Gallacher.

ROBERT 'BOBBY' FARRELL, c.1930

One of the most popular players to represent the club. Born in Dundee, he joined Brighton after a trial with Portsmouth and totted up, including war-time appearances, over 460 games in a long and distinguished career spanning fourteen years. A winger or inside-forward he scored 95 goals but made many more for his fellow forwards including Dan Kirkwood, Arthur Attwood, Alec Law and Bert Stephens. After giving up football Bobby was landlord of The Adur and Nevill public houses in Hove. He died in 1971.

FARRELL BRIGHTON & HOVE ALBION F.C.

OLD ALBION PROS V PRESS 1931.
WOODHOUSE. COOMBER. TOWNSEND. (AN OLD SUPPORTER) JENKINS. BOOTH. MEADS TRAINER
LONGSTAFF. MARSH. "BULLET" JONES. THOMPSON. MILLER. GROVES.

OLD BRIGHTON AND HOVE ALBION v. PRESS, 1931
A wealth of experience not to mention international and representative honours in this Albion line-up for a charity match. Such even ts were popular and useful money raisers. It is interesting to dwell on the prospects of such fixtures taking place in current day football. Certainly some old scores could be settled by ex-professionals and an abundance of red cards a distinct possibility!

PAUL MOONEY, 1931-32

Another long-serving player, Paul Mooney, arrived from East Stirling in 1925. A tall centre-half, he soon established himself after a handful of appearances in his first season. Dominant in the air, Paul retired in 1936 after over 300 games although he later played at Sussex County League level. Subsequently earned his living running The Wellington Hotel in College Place, Kemp Town, Brighton.

ERNEST KING, c.1931

A six-foot Londoner, full-back Ernie King arrived in 1931 from West Bromwich Albion. Only made one first team appearance in 1931-32 at Craven Cottage on 19th March 1932 when Fulham won 3-0, but established himself the following year and played over 200 times. Lost his place through injury in October 1937 and after that made only one more appearance, that in a F.A. Cup tie at Bury on 8th January 1938 which Brighton lost 2-0.

CUP-TIE SOUVENIR, 1933

Brighton's great cup run in 1932-33 did not have an auspicious start as the club secretary failed to claim exemption from the qualifying stages. Albion cruised through the early rounds defeating Shoreham (12-0), Worthing (7-1), Hastings & St Leonards (9-0) and Barnet (4-1). In the first round proper Crystal Palace were accounted for 2-1 followed by Wrexham. Then there was a great win over First Division Chelsea at the Goldstone. Bradford Park Avenue were the next victims at Hove and the Albion were into the fifth round and another home draw attracted a record 32,310 gate to watch the contest against West Ham. A terrific start saw Brighton go 2-0 up after twenty minutes. The Hammers came back strongly though to equalise and then win the replay with an extra time goal to deny Albion further cup glory.

DARLING. BRIGHTON & HOVE ALBION - 1933.

LEN DARLING, 1933

Born in Gillingham on 9th August 1911, Len Darling joined Brighton from the Kent club as a wing-half, stayed for fifteen years and in that span played 341 matches including 113 war-time appearances. His final game in an Albion shirt was in the home league match on 24th April 1948 when Notts County came out on top 3-1. The lone Brighton scorer was Tony James. The club finished bottom of the table and were forced to seek re-election for 1948-49. Len left to take up teaching but suffered from ill health and passed away in 1958.

JACK STEVENS, 1934

Stockport County transferred Jack Stevens to Brighton in the summer of 1934 and because of injuries was given an early opportunity in the first eleven. In 1935-36 he only missed two Division 3 (South) league matches at centre-half as Albion finished seventh in the table. Jack played nearly 150 games up to the outbreak of War and also assisted the club in war-time competition.

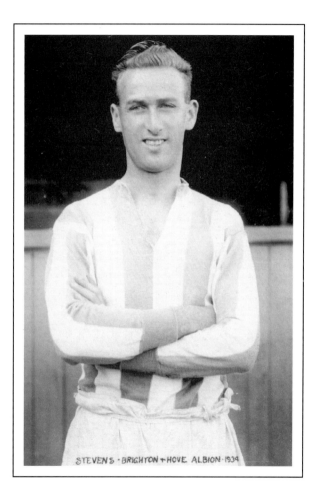

STEVENS · BRIGHTON & HOVE ALBION · 1934

BRIGHTON + HOVE ALBION

CUP-TIE TEAM 1935

MEADES (TRAINER). BROWN. THOMSON. MOONEY. KING. M? C.G.WEBB .(MANAGER)
FARRELL. JEPSON. JONES. WALKER. (DEANE WILES & MILLAR)
DARLING. POTTER SMITH. WILSON.

BRIGHTON AND HOVE ALBION, 1935

The line-up for the F.A. Cup 3rd round at the Goldstone against the mighty Arsenal on 12th January 1935. Having beaten Folkestone and Queens Park Rangers in earlier rounds this was a plum tie for Brighton, and although they lost 2-0 they were not disgraced in front of the 22,343 crowd. Arsenal included ten internationals in their team, amongst them Eddie Hapgood, Wilf Copping, Ted Drake and Cliff Bastin. Despite the defeat it was the highlight of the season for the Albion who could only finish ninth in Division 3 (South).

EDWARD MARTIN, c.1937

A full-back from Heanor Town, Ted Martin was born in Selston, Nottinghamshire. Joined Brighton in 1932 but did not gain a regular first team spot until the 1935-36 season. In his 155 league games for the Albion Ted scored four goals - all from the penalty spot. A further 65 appearances followed in war-time competition excluding the fixture at the Goldstone on 21st September 1940 when he was in the starting line-up to face Southampton. An air raid forced the game to be abandoned after 3¹/₂ minutes!

BRIGHTON AND HOVE ALBION, 1938-39

What was to be the last season of the Football League before the outbreak of the Second World War. Brighton finished third in Division 3 (South) behind Newport County and Crystal Palace, once again narrowly missing out on promotion. In the F.A. Cup Albion were knocked out in round one by non-league Yeovil. Line-up left to right -

Back row: Gordon Mee, Jack Philbin, Jock McNaughton, Charlie Thompson, Peter Trainor, Jock Davie.

Middle row: Bill Jones (asst. trainer), Bert Goffey, Freddie Green, Jack Stevens, Ernie Hall, Jimmy Cargill, Albert Day, Jack Atherton, Des Broomfield, Vic Saunders, Sam Cowan (trainer).

Front row: Alec Law, Ernie Marriott, Len Darling, Joe Wilson, Bob Vasey, Dave Walker (captain), Stan Risdon, Stan Hurst, Ted Martin, Bobby Farrell.

BRIGHTON NEW BOYS, 1938

Although there is a manuscript notation of 1939 on this postcard it is reasonable to suppose that the photo was taken in 1938 to introduce the new players prior to the start of the 1938-39 season. They are Peter Trainor and Jack Atherton from Preston North End, Jack Philbin and Freddie Green signed from Torquay, Bob Vasey (Notts County) and Albert Day. Their careers were interrupted due to the Second World War but Peter Trainor and Freddie Green were to continue with Brighton after the cessation of hostilities. Albert Day later played for Ipswich and Watford. Peter Trainor died in 1979.

WILF 'TIM' McCOY, c.1954
This postcard features Tim McCoy in his Tonbridge shirt subsequent to his Albion days. Born in Birmingham on 4th March 1921, he arrived at the Goldstone after periods with Portsmouth and Northampton Town. During his time at Brighton Tim was in competition with local product Alec South for the centre-half berth. Probably his best season was 1951-52 under new manager Billy Lane when he appeared in all bar four league matches and gave consistently solid performances to assist Brighton to fifth place in Division 3 (South).

DENNIS GORDON, c.1954
Another terrific servant of Brighton. Dennis, a right winger, predictably nicknamed "Flash". Born in Wolverhampton on 7th June 1924 he signed as a professional for West Bromwich Albion in September 1947 after moving from Oxford City. Transferring his allegiance South to the other Albion in July 1952 Dennis played over 290 league and cup games and was a member of the promotion winning side of 1957-58. Retired in 1961.

BRIGHTON v. BRISTOL CITY, 2nd October 1954
Jimmy Leadbetter getting in a shot on the Bristol City goal in the Division 3 (South) match which attracted 21,034 fans to the Goldstone. City won by the only goal from Jim Rogers and went on to take the title and earn promotion to Division 2. Brighton finished sixth in the table after recovering from a poor start. Jimmy Leadbetter was to leave the Albion at the end of that season for Ipswich where he gave sterling service to the Suffolk club until his retirement in 1964.

BRIGHTON AND HOVE ALBION, 1958-59

The line-up at the start of the 1958-59 season with the Third Division (South) Championship Shield, which they won at the end of 1957-58 so gaining promotion to Division 2 for the first time in the history of the club. Left to right -

Back row: Peter Harburn, Eric Hodge, Roy Jennings, Dave Hollins, Peter Rhodes, Alan Grant, Irvin Brown.

Third row: Tommy Bisset, Bernard Sibley, Dennis Gordon, Norman Stevens, Ken Whitfield, Glen Wilson (captain), Syd Ellis, John Shepherd, Steve Burtenshaw.

Second row: Joe Wilson (trainer), Keith Abbis, Ron Sleap, Jack Bertolini, Adrian Thorne, Des Tennant, Denis Foreman, Frankie Howard, Dave Sexton, Dennis Alexander, Cyril Hodges (assistant trainer).

Front row: Billy Lane (manager), Directors - Dr Alexander Greig, Arthur Pembroke, Gerald Paling, Alec Whitcher, General Sir Leslie Hollis and Harry Coverdale, Len Holt (secretary).

First choice goalkeeper Eric Gill is missing from the group.

FREDDIE JONES, c.1959
After Albion's shaky start to life in Division 2 in 1958-59, manager Billy Lane signed three new players to strengthen the side, Ronnie Clayton, Freddie Jones and shortly after Mike Tiddy. Also previously with Hereford Freddie and the other new signings helped Brighton to a respectable twelfth place. A left-winger, he scored in his second match in a 1-1 draw at Grimsby, and went on to play 76 games for the Albion and gain Welsh Under-23 honours. Transferred to Swindon Town in December 1960 and subsequently played for Grimsby and Reading.

DAVE TURNER, c.1963

Popular half-back Dave Turner was born in Retford on 7th September 1943. His first professional club was Newcastle before Albion manager Archie Macaulay signed him in December 1963 for a £6,000 fee. Despite injuries Dave played over 300 times and proved to be a bargain buy. Retired in 1973 after a season with Blackburn Rovers.

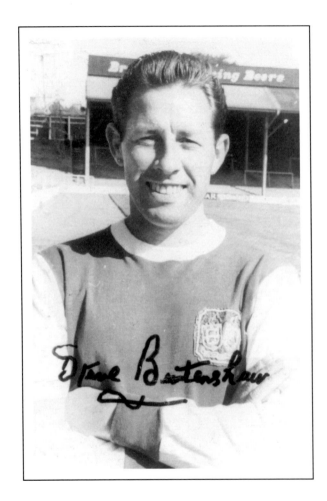

STEVE BURTENSHAW, c.1965

Born in Hove on 23rd November 1935, Steve Burtenshaw was one of three brothers to play league football. Charlie, who had assisted the Albion in wartime competition, and Bill were on Luton Town's books before moving to Gillingham. Steve was spotted playing for Brighton Boys and joined Albion's ground staff. A stylish wing-half whose fourteen year career at the Goldstone brought over 250 league and cup appearances. In the twilight of his career at the club Steve took on coaching duties. He also later coached at Arsenal and Everton and had a spell as manager of Sheffield Wednesday.

BRIGHTON AND HOVE ALBION, 1967-68
The team group at the start of the 1967-68 season. Players left to right are -
Back row: Brian Tawse, Stewart Henderson, Andy Tasker, Paul Bence, George Dalton,
Wally Gould, John Duncliffe, Paul Flood.
Middle row: Cyril Hodges (trainer), Charlie Livesey, Kit Napier, Roger Badminton, Brian Powney,
Tony Burns, Eric Whitington, John Templeman, Jimmy Magill, Steve Burtenshaw (coach).
Front row: Wilf Tranter, Norman Gall, Mike Hickman, Howard Wilkinson, Bob Fuller,
Jim Oliver, Stewart Ogden, Dave Turner (captain).
Late signings not in the group were John Napier from Bolton and Nobby Lawton, Preston North End.
Brighton disappointed and finished tenth in Division 3 after a mediocre season.

CHRISTOPHER 'KIT' NAPIER,
c.1969

Born in Dunblane, Scotland, on 26th September 1943, a Schoolboy international who arrived at Brighton via Blackpool, Preston North End, Workington and Newcastle. Signed for £9,000 by Archie Macaulay Kit was an immediate success scoring twice on his debut on 1st October 1966 against Peterborough at the Goldstone. Wally Gould netted two and Dave Turner was also on target as the Albion surged to a 5-2 victory despite being 1-0 down at the halfway poin t. A skilful forward Kit scored 99 goals in 284 league and cup appearances before a transfer took him to Blackburn Rovers in August 1972.

JOHN NAPIER, c.1969

Another Napier joined Brighton in August 1967. Born in Northern Ireland (23rd September 1946) a then record £25,000 fee brought John, a central defender, from Bolton Wanderers. His consistent performances made him the first recipient of the Player of the Year award in 1968-69. Made over 100 consecutive appearances from February 1970 to March 1972. A Northern Ireland international, he totalled almost 250 games for the Albion before a transfer in October 1972 to Bradford City.

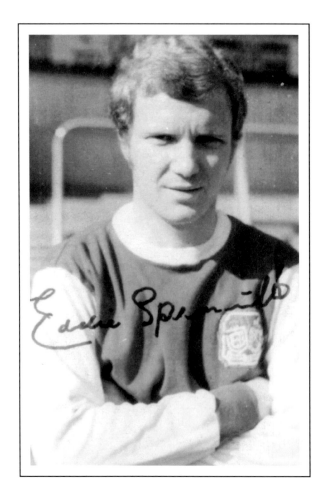

EDDIE SPEARRITT, c.1969

Voted Player of the Season in 1972-73, Lowestoft born Eddie Spearritt was a £20,000 capture from Ipswich. Made his Brighton debut on 25th January 1969 days before his 22nd birthday, when Crewe were beaten 3-1 at the Goldstone with goals from Dave Armstrong, Kit Napier and Alex Dawson. A long throw specialist Eddie was ever present in the promotion winning side of 1971-72, and was appointed club captain in 1973-74. Was transferred to Carlisle in June 1974 after over 200 games for Albion and later also played for Gillingham.

NORMAN GALL, c.1971

Norman was signed from Gateshead in March 1962. Born in Wallsend on 30th September 1942 he was another of the players like Dave Turner who formed the backbone of the side in the sixties and were automatic choices on the team sheet. Played in every league match in defence in 1971-72 when Albion gained promotion to Division 2 along with champions Aston Villa. Appearances in league and cup totalled 474 and was voted Player of the Season by the fans in 1970-71 and 1973-74.

Bert Murray

BERT MURRAY, c.1971

Albion under new manager, Pat Saward, had a disappointing start to the 1970-71 season. With lack of funds to buy new players the manager was forced to appeal for money from supporters to assist his search for fresh faces. Proceeds from sponsored walks and other events enabled him to acquire the services of Bert Murray from Birmingham City, who became known as "The People's Player". This capture and other loan signings helped Brighton to finish in a respectable league position. Bert was to play over 100 games for the club before moving on in 1973.

STEVE PIPER, c.1972

Brighton born Steve Piper signed professional terms in September 1972 two months before his nineteenth birthday after a spell on the ground staff. A central defender, he made over 180 appearances in Albion colours. Scored an important goal in the 3-2 home win over Sheffield Wednesday on 3rd May 1977 which clinched promotion to the Second Division for Brighton. Other goals came from Peter Ward and a Brian Horton penalty. A transfer took Steve along the coast to Portsmouth in February 1978.

BRIAN CLOUGH
AND PETER TAYLOR

Brighton chairman Mike Bamber pulled off a masterstroke when he acquired the services of Brian Clough and Peter Taylor as manager and assistant manager respectively in October 1973 to replace the sacked Pat Saward. A 4-0 home defeat in the F.A. Cup at the hands of non-league Walton and Hersham plus an 8-2 drubbing by Bristol Rovers at the Goldstone in front of T.V. cameras left the new management in no doubt that wholesale changes were necessary. By July 1974 Brian Clough had departed to Leeds but Peter Taylor stayed to continue the rebuilding and Albion narrowly missed out on promotion to Division 2 in 1975-76. The postcard is a limited edition of 1,000 published by Reflections of a Bygone Age to commemorate the continued success of the Clough-Taylor partnership at Nottingham Forest.

PETER O'SULLIVAN, c.1977

A nineteen year old midfield player joined Brighton from Manchester United in April 1970. Peter O'Sullivan was to be a vital part of the team over the next ten years, always probing and creating chances for his forwards. A Welsh schoolboy international, Peter also gained under-23 and full international caps for his outstanding club performances. His appearances for the Seagulls totalled 488, a record second only to Tug Wilson's in the twenties and thirties. Towards the end of his career moved to Fulham, Charlton, Reading and Aldershot as well as playing in California and Hong Kong.

THE GOLDSTONE GROUND, 1979

This postcard was issued to commemorate Brighton's first ever match in the First Division against Arsenal on 18th August 1979 at the Goldstone. A memorable day for the 28,604 spectators despite the fact that the Seagulls lost 4-0 and were given a lesson in finishing. After a poor start the Albion eventually found their feet in the exalted company and finished in sixteenth place in the table. The small stand with the white roof was a temporary extension to the West Stand which provided a further 980 seats. It was nicknamed the Lego Stand and was demolished in 1985.

PETER WARD, c.1979

Probably the most exciting player to wear a Brighton shirt. A forward costing £4,000 from Burton Albion in May 1975, he scored 50 seconds after his first team debut on 27th March 1976. The following season saw him forge a great partnership with Ian Mellor and become the leading goalscorer in the Football League, surpassing the previous club record of 32 set by Hugh Vallance, with a 36 goal tally. On 6th September 1977 Peter represented England Under-21 at the Goldstone Ground and scored a hat-trick. Transferred to Nottingham Forest for £400,000 in October 1980, he did return to the Seagulls on loan briefly during the 1982-83 season. Later continued his football in the United States and now runs a public house in Florida.

BRIGHTON AND HOVE ALBION, 1983

One of the highlights in the history of the club was reaching the F.A. Cup final in 1983, despite losing 4-0 in a replay after holding Manchester United to a 2-2 draw in the first encounter. Brighton could have won this first match in extra time but for that infamous miss by Gordon Smith. Albion, sponsored by British Caledonian, are the only finalists to arrive at Wembley by helicopter. A holiday in California followed and shown above are the players enjoying the sunshine outside George Best's nightclub. Unfortunately 1982-83 saw the Seagulls lose their First Division status.